Poetry is Life
Writing with Yellow Arrow

A book of poems and ideas compiled by Ann Quinn

Kapua Iao, Editor-in-Chief
Alexa Laharty, Creative Director
Angela Firman, Editorial Associate
Rachel Vinyard, Editorial Associate

with additional editing by Linda Gail Francis

Cover art by Claudia Cameron

Interior photographs from Linda Gail Francis, Patrick W. Gibson, Rose Ocone, Ann Quinn, and Jobie Townshend-Zellner

Contributors

Linda Gail Francis, Patrick W. Gibson, Jessica Gregg,
Sara Palmer, Julia W. Prentice, Patti Ross,
Nikita Rimal Sharma, and Jobie Townshend-Zellner

D1216228

YELLOW ARROW
PUBLISHING
Baltimore, MD 21057
info@yellowarrowpublishing.com

Library of Congress Control Number: 2022930476
ISBN (paperback): 978-1-7350230-9-0

Cover art ("Coastal Vibrancy") by Claudia Cameron
(claudiacameron.smugmug.com; Instagram @claudiaocameron).
Interior design by Yellow Arrow Publishing.

For more information, see yellowarrowpublishing.com.

We prioritize the unique voice and style of each of our authors.

Every writer has a story to tell and every story is worth telling.

Yellow Arrow Publishing

Table of Contents

Acknowledgments

I would like to thank my mentors in poetry, particularly Nan Fry and Lia Purpura, for inspired teaching that I am privileged to pass on, and my student-mentors who make up this wonderful class of poets. Much gratitude to everyone at Yellow Arrow Publishing, especially Kapua, for her tireless work on behalf of writers. And to the reader: thank you for your eyes and your words. They are important.

Dear Readers,

The first time I was published in *Yellow Arrow Journal* (Vol. IV, No. 1, **DOUBT**), I was asked to create a prompt for readers based on my process in writing the included poem "Tritina for My Grandmother." What a cool idea, to involve the reader as writer! As I got more involved with Yellow Arrow Publishing, I saw more and more innovative, inclusive ideas like this, and when Gwen Van Velsor, Yellow Arrow's founder, asked if I would like to teach a year-long poetry class, I was in. That was over two years ago. Our first class was held in person at Yellow Arrow House, in Highlandtown, Baltimore in March 2020. In April of 2020 we went to Zoom and haven't looked back—saying goodbye to friends from all over the country is not an option.

A few days before each class, I send out four or five poems in advance—typically poems by well-known writers that exemplify the theme we will work on. We then begin class by discussing one of the poems, sussing out how the writer did it—how the poem works for the reader, and how the writer might have gotten to the final product. I give a prompt and we set to writing for 10 or 15 minutes. We then come back and share what we've written. We repeat this process two or three times, with different poems and prompts.

All the work that you'll read in this volume came from those classes. While you won't have the experience of talking with us about the model poems, you will get to see how class poets worked with the prompts. Nearly all the poems mentioned in the text are available online, and I hope that they will inspire you to get some books and spend more time with these poets. Mostly, I hope that they will inspire you to write your own life.

Ann Quinn

Ann Quinn
Class Instructor and Poetry Editor

January

Write of the Ordinary

What to read:

Ursula K. Le Guin, "Kitchen Spoons"
Pablo Neruda, "Ode to My Socks"
Nancy Willard, "A Wreath to the Fish"

*P*oetry elevates the ordinary, making us realize that in a sense, there is nothing truly ordinary. Things have histories, and poems can bring those histories to light. We began this month with Ursula K. Le Guin's "Kitchen Spoons" (not available on the Internet), from her collection *Late in the Day*, in which an old spoon and a new spoon tell their stories. The old spoon is from "our first apartment, on Holt Avenue in Macon, Georgia, in 1954, the downstairs of widow Killian's house." We conjure a world from Le Guin's description of this spoon.

Sara conjures a world in her poem; what everyday objects in your life have a story to tell?

PROMPT

Find an ordinary object that has some special place in your life history—something you use, every day or nearly every day (not your computer). Write the story of your object with lots of detail—don't worry too much about poetic lines or even concise language. Get it all down; you can edit later.

My Father-in-Law's Coffee Grinder
Sara Palmer

Poppy Red, popular in kitchens
back in the years of marching
against the war in Vietnam, when
Nixon resigned, and the Reds
carried the day.

Countless mornings
the grinding buzz of its blade
drowned out those headlines,
declaring instead the start
of your day's routine:
breakfast, then down the stairs
to your dental office
where patients waited
for the buzz of your drill.

Now that red grinder sits
on my modern gray granite
kitchen counter,
quaintly out of place
small and squat but oh-so-bold.
Pieces of the plastic top
are broken away
from overuse and yet
the white electric cord is
smooth, the blades turn
just like new.

Inside, the residue of beans
stains the steel bowl brown,
and fragrant remnants
of yesterday's grind
remind me how we moved

from strangers to family,
coffee easing the awkwardness
percolating between us,
caffeine making us playful.

You tried to drink me under the table,
but back then I could buzz
and buzz, no limits.
Conversations flowed faster
with each cup consumed,
in your kitchen or mine—
you in your prime
and me, so young.

Every sip brought us closer
to the love that later
made me want to care for you
until, after decades, I was left alone
in your empty apartment
in northwest Baltimore
giving away your last possessions,
finding the old red grinder,
saving it for myself.

Write of the Ordinary

*N*ancy Willard brings magic to the ordinary. We read "A Wreath to the Fish" and talked about the role of questions in poetry and how to let the magic in.

After some revision, in which questions came out of the draft, Patti completed the following poem, first published in the Oyster River Pages *Composite Dreams* issue.

PROMPT

Write about something organic (food or garbage or a creature. . . .), repeating the question, "Who is this _____?" Bring something of magic to the item.

Praise for Colewort
(green leafy plant of the species Brassica)

Patti Ross

Hallowed the scent of pig's feet
lining street corners mowed
with empty-bellied hounds
forestalling fate of roadkill

Croon to wet basements
poverty's stench where clothes hang
evading theft and downpour
Glade tames the damp and vermin

Revere relief of anxiety
the fragrance of peace
Hallelujah!
Holy are the collard greens

I couldn't let this class pass without a reading of Pablo Neruda's "Ode to My Socks." If you don't know that poem, please go read it right now.

Pat came up with a wonderful remembrance of something as ordinary as socks, and yet extraordinary, because it was worn by someone special.

PROMPT

»———➤

Write an ode to something everyday.

Purple Parka
Patrick W. Gibson

As a child she never left the house
in winter
without her purple parka.
Its sleeves shrunk against
her extended arms.
Its hood bound in plastic fur
provided little warmth
but framed her scarlet hair.
Its zippered front missing
a tooth or two
in compliment of its owner.
And lest I forget its pockets
split open at the seams, cradling
brown paper sandwich bags,
Sharpied with messages
have a nice day
reinforced with
happy faced exclamations.
And within each lay
mummified remains:
cheese sandwich,
white bread,
no butter,
crust removed,
just right
like that parka
and its owner
ripe with secrets.

February

Persona

What to read:

Louise Glück, "Abishag"
Marilyn Nelson, *Sweethearts of Rhythm*

*O*ne of the best things about being a poet is that you can be anything or anyone on the page. It's more than fun because you will learn so much about yourself by inhabiting another's voice. Take a look at Louise Glück's "Abishag," in which we get the point of view of the young woman chosen to lie chastely with the dying King David, solely to keep him warm. Glück has given Abishag voice, and dreams, and you can do this, too.

Sara took on the biblical character of Sarah in her poem.

PROMPT

Write from the point of view of a character—biblical, historical, or mythological, from a fairy tale or even a favorite book. You might shake the character into the present by casting your poem in the form of an email, or a text, or a tweet.

Sarah Says Her Piece
Sara Palmer

Oh, Abraham, you silly
old man! You thought I was
laughing?! Does a woman laugh,
at my age, when she learns
she's with child? True,
I threw back my head,
and a sound flew from
my throat: half-strangling,
half-bellowing, a moan
careening back through
decades of denial. But
that was no laugh.

Why now, in my dotage,
long past the smoldering rage
I felt as Hagar paraded her
Ishmael under my nose,
long past the time when
wombs shrivel and women
embrace their barrenness?

(God, your warped sense of humor,
your reasons, I will never comprehend.
You do what you do.)

Nevertheless, he was born,
our Isaac. You named him
for laughter. It wasn't funny
between you two. You took him
up the mountain on false pretenses

(did you even **once** think to ask
my opinion?) Lucky for me
the angel appeared to flutter
her wings and tell you
there'd been a change of plans.
Too bad for the ram, though.

Oh, Abraham, you wavering weakling,
what did you think? That he'd come
back to us after that performance?
Not on your life. Isaac was long gone
by the time you saddled your ass
to head home.

However, he survived, our Izzy.
I often picture him, spiraling down
the mountain, racing his way
toward a life without you.
That's when I throw back my head,
and I laugh.

Persona

*Y*ou can also write persona from the point of view of a thing. Marilyn Nelson does this brilliantly in her book *Sweethearts of Rhythm*, in which the instruments played by members of an all-women touring jazz band speak in individual poems.

Jessica did a timely riff on this shortly after the insurrection of January 6, 2021, by writing from the point of view of that infamous coonskin hat worn by the painted, shirtless, much-photographed person. Rather than trying to take on the whole political mess, she writes from the specific point of view of this humble hat. Her poem was subsequently published in *Delmarva Review*.

PROMPT

Give an inanimate object voice on your page.

The Horned Hat at the Insurrection

Jessica Gregg

Stitched by minnow fingers
pebble-skipping over tufted
fake fur, one of oh-so-many,
I confess I was meant
for a stage smaller than this.
A community production
of O, Pioneers, perhaps?
God, look at me, I grand marshal
this snake train of tobacco-
stained, piss-scented
would-be Vikings,
the haberdashery helming
a pinwheel platform.
Circling parquet corridors
with flags and the false GPS
of rigged moral compasses,
oh, they are indeed pioneers.
Bow hunters—Antaeus waiting
for a fistfight, forging ground
on hallowed ground.
Glory, I could have been a mascot,
a bombastic bison, big horned,
bugling, canon-shot badassery,
not the taxidermy footnote
in the unraveling of democracy.

March

Poems of Address

What to read:

William Blake, "To the Evening Star"
Ann Quinn, "To the Waxed Red Delicious at My Local King Soopers"

*H*ow fun, as a poet, that we get to talk to things on paper, whether or not they know that we exist! We began this month by reading "To the Evening Star" by William Blake.

Well, the first bright light in the sky is usually Venus, and Patti put her own spin on that orb.

PROMPT

Write your own poem to the evening star.

Venus the Feminist
Patti Ross

I love your golden glimmer.
Your bright light
reminds me of that black girl magic
I dream each night.

I like how you trek your own path.
Did you flip the script on purpose?
Did you do it to avoid the mass?

Your aged beauty, that of a Goddess.
An equally sculptured outline.
I understand why Uranus almost flipped
and follows behind.

You were right not to have any moons.
Nothing to take away your bright shine.
After all, we never needed rings
to show our love.

*N*ext, I shared my own poem, "To the Waxed Red Delicious at My Local King Soopers." You can find a reading of this online, via the *Little Patuxent Review's* YouTube channel.

Jobie found a perfect set of objects to address.

PROMPT

»———➔

Address something that symbolizes something you object to in some way. Not a person but perhaps an object belonging to a person, such as a hat or a sign. Now write a poem to that object, without overtly judging it. You'll notice a tie-in to the Persona chapter—in poetry we can be the thing or we can talk to the thing. Poetry makes us feel powerful!

Wooden Boxes of January 6, 2021
Jobie Townshend-Zellner

You three boxes unfolded history today, due
to your contents. On this day, your invisibility dissolved
as television and Internet viewers witnessed
your controversial role in congressional halls.

The tallest of you brown shiny wooden boxes
hovered over you smaller ones like a big brother.
You all were firmly secured—two vertical leather-like straps
buckled in your contents, and a third circled your mid-sections.
But before you finished your silent civic duty
you were unceremoniously picked up by your handles
and whisked away with exiting lawmakers.

Later you were ushered back into the chamber.
You didn't look bent out of shape at all.
Your visages had no ponderosity
nor the jawboning of elected officials.
Calmly you stood while Mike Pence finished roll call
for your ordinary quadrennial event, which became
an epiphany of sorts for the rest of the nation!

April

Myth & Fairy Tale

What to read:

Michael Collier, "Argus"
Louise Glück, many books and poems
Andrea Hollander, "Gretel"
Lisel Mueller, "Immortality"
Linda Pastan, "You are Odysseus"

*Y*ou'll also see characters from myth and the Bible in our chapters on persona (February) and poems of address (March). We want to interact with these larger-than-life characters. And they're part of our common language. Another topic for poetry is our own relationship with well-known stories. We read Michael Collier's "Argus," in which the speaker, reading the story of Odysseus again, later in life, is drawn to the dog Argus, overlooked in his earlier reading. We also read "You are Odysseus" by Linda Pastan, in which she sees her marriage in light of the story—she thought she was a siren, but perhaps after all she is Penelope. Other poems to look at are "Immortality" by Lisel Mueller, "Gretel" by Andrea Hollander, and many poems and books by Louise Glück.

PROMPT

Write yourself into a myth or fairy tale. Use the name of the story or the character only in the title. In the poem, let the reader make the connections for themselves.

Green Peas and a Princess
Jessica Gregg

The tunnel was backed up; by the time
she reached the beach house, the sky
above the Assawoman Bay had swallowed
the sun. They welcomed her in, their tanned
grips, Chardonnay smiles, a receiving line
of look-alikes looking her over. She brought
cantaloupe, peach pie, and snap peas bought
at a roadside stand marooned in corn stalks.
They installed her in the boathouse, beneath
wood beams that made her feel below deck.
She was, in fact, two and a half stories above
sea level, above the jellyfish-filled slate waters,
in eaves where up seemed down, down seemed up,
and without a compass, could no longer find
her bearings. Meanwhile, the hero—her hero
—unzipped the peas and macheted into the melon,
cleaving its juicy flesh into two moons the family
ate the next morning as she overslept, dreaming
of sliding through the briny, enchanted waters
slapping against the boathouse and its dock.

May

Mothers & Grandmothers

What to read:

Eavan Boland, *A Woman Without a Country* and
"Studio Portrait 1897"
Michael Collier, "Grandmother with Mink Stole, Sky Harbor
Airport, Phoenix, Arizona, 1959"
Rita Dove, *Thomas and Beulah* and "Sunday Greens"
Carolyn Forché, "The Morning Baking"
Natasha Trethewey, *Domestic Work*

*M*emories of mothers and grandmothers are a rich mine for poet-telling. In May, we began with "The Morning Baking" by Carolyn Forché, from her first book, *Gathering the Tribes*.

Often we'll start a poem with words from another poet, and then once our own words and thoughts have come together, we can drop the other poet's words. It's a bit like using a sourdough starter you get from a friend or relative to make your own nourishment. Here's the finished bread (I mean poem) that Patti baked from Forché's starter. This poem appeared in the online zine *The Rising Phoenix River Review*.

PROMPT

Begin a poem with the words:

(Mother/Grandmother/Nana, etc.) come back
I forgot _____.

My West African Grandmother
Patti Ross

I hope to go to Senegal

To see Lac Rose
a pink piscine of salt
sun beaten and gummy.

I linger shoreside and watch
my guide Ahmed rubs Shea butter
over his full body, gliding into the sticky mer.
The everyday work of the poor.
Salt catchers!

I am reminded how mama sifted
boiled dough into a small pot of butter
in preparation for the salty bean broth.

I should go to Goree Island.
Visit the Maison des Esclaves and
see the white sand beaches, the palm trees
contrasting the echo of screams
from a door swinging solely one way.

I must go to Bargny and watch
Mother Fatou
smoke the fish in small concrete tombs
filled with fire and ash,
daily the air heavy and grave on her lungs.

They are replacing the tombs now
furnaces, modern not aged
no smoke, no ash, no tumeur maligne.
Will the Thieboudienne taste the same?
Jollof rice and fish with no tang of smoke?

I want to meet my grandmother,
who has aged and is dying,
her salty bean broth,
the smell of smoked fish
a family heirloom.

I hope to go to Senegal.

Mothers & Grandmothers

*N*ext we read Michael Collier's "Grandmother with Mink Stole, Sky Harbor Airport, Phoenix, Arizona, 1959" and talked about how the incredible sensory detail along with the title evoke a particular time and place. Notice that we get five stanzas describing the stole; just one describing the grandmother. And yet we get a strong sense of what she was like, in this slant description.

Linda, instead of choosing one item, chose the lifestyle of her mother's sewing, but see how the detail helps us imagine her mother's sewing room, and revel in where it led the poet in this poem.

PROMPT

Choose an item of clothing that you associate with your forebear. Begin by describing it in excruciating detail, including how and where it was worn and see where it leads you.

Patterns

Linda Gail Francis

Fat quarters and scraps of cotton,
calico, batik, plaids, vibrant florals
arranged in stacks by shade
fill my mother's sewing room
to the ceiling, and pinned along the wall,
squares and flowers in the making,
patterns and sketches, spools of thread
placed neatly on pegs,
hopeful elements of future quilts.

Although she tried, I learned no skill
at sewing one side and knowing, then,
how it will look when turned back out,
how dangerous the bias, easily misjudged.
It's hard to sew an even stitch,
even by machine, then rip it out,
bunched and wrong. But, far away,
I join her in that room when I poem
as she quilts, select from a world of words
just a few, place, replace,
and rearrange to some effect,
our work not done until we say.

*N*ikita wrote this shimmering poem, beginning with the colors her mother wears each day. This will be published in her debut chapbook, *The most beautiful garden*, published in 2022 by Yellow Arrow Publishing.

The most beautiful garden
Nikita Rimal Sharma

My Taa dresses up everyday,
in the brightest shades of yellow and red.
"You are dressed like a garden," I say.

And a garden she is,
perhaps a bed of lotus,
with muddy foundations of patriarchy.

Or maybe she has morphed into
a fragrant bush of roses—
enamored by beauty,
guarded by thorns.

*I*f you'd like to write poetry about your family's matrilineal history, I highly recommend Eavan Boland's *A Woman Without a Country*, Natasha Tretheway's *Domestic Work*, and Rita Dove's *Thomas and Beulah*.

I think that Sara's poem "In the Kitchen circa 1939" shows the influence of two poems we read together: Boland's "Studio Portrait 1897" and Dove's "Sunday Greens." Because Sara chose to keep the anaphora from Dove's poem, she mentions Dove below the title. It is always OK to borrow inspiration from another's poem, and if the resemblance is discernible, just credit the original poet. It shows that you are a part of this worldwide community of poets.

PROMPT

>>———→

Write about your forebear in the third person, without naming them, in their daily life, beginning with the anaphora "She wants" stated at least three times.

In the Kitchen circa 1939
Sara Palmer

After Rita Dove

She wants to wear a white apron
like Betty Crocker, baking her pies.
She bows her head
over the saucepan, acrid
sweetness filling her nose:
her lemon custard
coming
to a boil.

She wants to sing
"God Bless America"
while her hands perform
a symphony of Thanksgiving
feats: chopping, grinding,
tearing
stale bread
to pieces.

She beats the egg whites
without mercy, until
their stiff peaks stand up
to the photos in her magazine.
Spreading the meringue,
she might forget
she was foreign-born,
her mother fleeing
a Russian shtetl, bringing
only her children;

she might forget her father's
absence that
sealed
their poverty.

She wants to wave
an American flag
like a magic wand that wipes
away traces of her past;
to melt into a faceless pot,
and fill her children's ears
with the roar of a cheering
crowd, never to let them
hear words
simmering
with hate:

Dirty immigrant.
Kike.
Pinko.

She doesn't want her children
to know where she was raised:
the Jewish Orphans Asylum,
a place to chop off her roots,
force new shoots, to grow
into safety,
become
a citizen.

They taught her English
with a Cleveland accent,
gave her a high school diploma,

showed her how to wear
button-front dresses,
stack-heeled shoes,
to place a string
of pearls
around
her throat.

She doesn't want to change
her clothes with the times,
prefers to shelter inside
this once-modern ensemble.
She wears it now,
in the kitchen
under her white apron,
cooking New World dishes
to feed her American children.
She gives thanks. They will never
feel the endless
pangs
of her immigrant
hunger.

June

Fathers

What to read:

Reginald Dwayne Betts, "Blood History"
Billy Collins, "Death of a Hat"
Susan Rich, "The Photograph Suggests a Hidden Life"
Rainer Maria Rilke, "Portrait of my Father as a Young Man"

*F*athers inspire their share of poetry. We read Rainer Maria Rilke's "Portrait of my Father as a Young Man," Susan Rich's "The Photograph Suggests a Hidden Life," and Reginald Dwayne Betts' "Blood History." This prompt was inspired by Billy Collins' "Death of a Hat."

PROMPT

Think of something your father wore or collected or did that has fallen out of fashion. Write a poem about that. Let your father enter later into the poem, but only a little.

Suits

Patti Ross

I do like the buttons with their tiger eye petition—
they add a point of superiority. The wide lapel
at first seems vast
yet it gives merit to the look.
I like the army green one best.
The beige one has the characteristic of stylish.

Father, you make those leisure suits look elegant.
I often wondered where you bought them.
Franco's in downtown Richmond?
Had I seen one in the front window display,
or was it a gentleman's store up north?
Bought while you were doing business for freedom?

I loved the few times you let me tag along.
My eyes watching you move the fabric
between your fingers, ensuring its quality.
I remember once you asked about the stitching,
whether hand or machine done. Then reminding me
to look at the details and how life is the same
as a good suit. The details tell the story.

When grandmother and I would walk past the
downtown stores, I imagined that you were inside.
You were trying on the latest style or color.
You were there asking the clerk about the make and design.
You were near.

Once while we were waiting there
on the bubblegum sprayed sidewalk,
I dreamed you were coming to pick us up
in your new baby blue Ford Thunderbird. I was hungry
and we would have lunch downtown. On the bus
ride back home, for the first time I noticed
the torn seams in the seats and the coldness of the fabric.
I tried to feel the quality of it but there was a numbness instead.
I started to wonder what details tell my story
and if I will ever wear an army green suit.

Fathers

*N*ow Julia's poem—I must admit that this was related to a different prompt, in which we wrote about objects in the room around us, but you see how the details work to show us something about this man. Julia's room contains many things that remind her of her father, who was an antiquarian book dealer.

Illuminated Manuscript
Julia W. Prentice

In the North, a compass points to time long past
While turntable scratches out beloved opera;
Catalogues with illuminated letters stand open
Warm golds, gilt silver, carmine and royal
Black italics, ink flowing, line after line.

In the West, the brown spaniel's ears perk
As its liquid eyes gaze raptly at the old
Wooden bird feeder he patiently filled with
Black oil sunflower seeds. See the cardinal,
Preening feathers and chirping,
Ignoring his red sweater while he putters?

Moving South, see his apple-tinted tool chest
Sharp and dangerous soldering iron and
Bandsaw that whines, grating ears and heart.
His black fur hat still hangs on the hat rack,
Coat draped casually on a cozy wicker chair.

In the East, sun breaks over the red brick house
White trim, and neat green boxwood hedges,
Except where he forgot to clip:
Twin magnolias and tallest pines are
Witnesses to what still lingers. . . .

Operatic airs on the breeze,
Old leather and antiquarian ink on vellum,
Cardinal's saddest song: 'what cheer?'
Oily tools and soft wool coat,
Scent of magnolia blossoms and pine.

July

Image

What to read:

Elizabeth Bishop, "At the Fishhouses"
Stanley Kunitz, "The Round"
Ada Limón, "Instructions on Not Giving Up"
Mary Oliver, *A Poetry Handbook*

*I*mage is a huge, important topic for poets. So far we've only devoted one session to it, but I suspect there will be more. I sent the class the "Image" chapter from Mary Oliver's essential book, *A Poetry Handbook* (and yes, you can find the PDF online but I encourage you to purchase and spend time with your own paper copy). We read Elizabeth Bishop's "At the Fishhouses" and Stanley Kunitz's "The Round," which are both reprinted in Oliver's book. We also read Ada Limón's amazing "Instructions on Not Giving Up." Then we wrote.

I love how Jobie lets the form of the poem mimic her aunt's orderly life in the first stanza and her family's looser style in the second by her choice of line spacing.

PROMPT

Have an interesting plant or shell or stone nearby to write about in depth. Write down a 10-minute description without image—use no simile or metaphor, just stick with dry scientific description. You will be surprised at how difficult this is.

Next, write a 10-minute personification of the same thing. Let the metaphor run wild.

Now, look at a poem you have already written and see if an image could help the poem. Weave the image in.

Thresholds for Tea
Jobie Townshend-Zellner

On an upper shelf of Great Aunt Elena's hutch
sat a most delicate tea set—as diminutive and refined
as she, in whose Palo Alto condominium home
every thing had a place. Like her teacups fit into their saucers
people visiting only belonged in one place—on her couch
behind the rectangular coffee table—and only at teatime.

Never did I witness her tea ceremony, for it seemed

a travesty of family ties to our mother whom I never saw

worship at her aunt's altar of tradition.

Our mother and dad's front door was most often

open for friends and family members comfortable

with our largely improvised home life.

We indeed served guests tea—straight from the kitchen

in cups or mugs—to any part of our home, the threshold of which

no porcelain tea set had ever dared to cross.

*A*nd Julia wrote a sonnet with images of volcanoes and castles within the image of the bromeliad's secret.

Bromeliad

Julia W. Prentice

With spears of green those swords are pointed sharp
As a finished blade. Twenty stand and arc
Up and out flaring fiercest green, to guard
Its sweet flower nestling, hiding inward
Circled by its glowing petals, jewels
They turn red to orange like lava cools
On mountain tops. Bromeliad within
Grows inside its planter wrought from tin
A shiny metal castle, its ramparts
Lean outward in defense of tender heart.
Watering can is raining down, weeping
Heart throbs while roots so deep are keeping

A secret, resting beneath the softest soil
New bud, it swells to nature's urgent bell.

August

Prose Poems are Confusing

What to read:

Robert Hass, "A Story About the Body"
David Ignatow, "I'm a Depressed Poem"
Amy Lowell, "Bath"
Francis Ponge, "The Frog" (translated)

*P*rose poems are confusing—what makes them poems? What's the difference between a prose poem and flash fiction or nonfiction? My answer: if it's in a book or journal of poetry, it's a poem. If it's in a book or journal of fiction or nonfiction, it's that. In other words, there is no clear line. Just write using amazing language and make it worth reading. Prose poems we read: "The Frog" by Francis Ponge (translated), "I'm a Depressed Poem" by David Ignatow, "A Story About the Body" by Robert Hass, and "Bath" by Amy Lowell.

Can there be too many cat poems? I think not.

PROMPT

Write a prose poem description of an animal, referring to a photo for details, unless you have an animal at hand. Give the animal a gender and include at least two instances of personification. Begin with a description of a movement (you can make this up if you need to) and include two metaphors. Keep it under 110 words (approximately; don't spend time counting).

Catlyn

Julia W. Prentice

She flops, then rolls, belly to sky, rubs her cheek to rug in abandon, blissful indulgence of kitten-play. With her fur speckled, freckled, mottled with stripes of black on golden brown, and tabby spots on muscled shoulders that move and undulate beneath that pelt. Chin tilted upward awaiting scratches, feathered whiskers twitch, while rose-pink nose wrinkles triangular. Lime-green eyes bat bewitchingly. Sunlight sets soft fur aglow, golden sheen like melted butter. Tail never still, always swishing at the tip, hunting butterflies in drowsy dreams.

September

List Poems

What to read:

N. Scott Momaday, "The Delight Song of Tsoai-talee"
Walt Whitman, "I Hear America Singing"

*W*e read Walt Whitman's "I Hear America Singing." We read N. Scott Momaday's "The Delight Song of Tsoai-talee." We talked about the power of (Write it!) detail and anaphora—that chorus of repetition that makes a poem become like a prayer.

Linda managed to do both in this powerful poem. Notice how the details gather power as they accumulate.

PROMPT

Write an "I Hear" or "I Am" poem.

I am

Linda Gail Francis

I am
clean laundry piled on the bed,
fresh from the tumble-dry;
the infection in my cat's ear;
the chimes awakening to the breeze
in the open window;
the work computer, still at home.
I am this strange America, this old house;
the distraction, the argument, the virus, the variant;
a September morning walk in the park;
the lawn mower, weed whacker.
I am the insistent cricket in a choir of cicadas;
the little black car with darkened windows
that barrels through the street.
I hear the crash that is going to happen one day.

October

One Sentence Poems

What to read:

*O*ne sentence poems are powerful. It is amazing what you can get into one sentence—sometimes virtuosically, like in Terrence Hayes' "Carp Poem," or sometimes more simply, like in Tracy K. Smith's "The Good Life." Either way, forcing yourself to keep a thought going can be magic for writing a good poem, one that sweeps the reader along.

PROMPT

Write a poem about when you were younger, possibly starting with "When people. . . ." Make it one fluid, grammatical sentence.

Social Driftwood
Jobie Townshend-Zellner

When some people talk about being engaged

to be wed, they sound like they've found

the perfect picture frame to surround

their expanding lives

and I recall a one week engagement

I endured, as if seeing jail cell

bars slowly begin to close, and

all I knew was to kick myself

back into a framework of honesty

and break the news as gently as a breeze

that this chosen periphery

was not for me, trusting that

other life-framing devices would

surface, like driftwood on the sand

that could be suitably transformed for me,

for him, for all the social drifters.

Sara found another way to begin her poem, but see how the form is perfect for the wobbly nonstopping of a first real bike ride?

PROMPT

Read Edward Hirsch's "The Baker Swept By." Write a poem addressed to "you" about a moment in the past. It might start with "When." See if you can bring one image back into the poem two or three times.

Leaving
Sara Palmer

You were just beginning
to ride the used blue bicycle
Daddy bought you (used like his
cars—clunkers he called them—
because why spend money on a bike
you'd outgrow in a year),
and the day Daddy let you
take off the training wheels
and ride down the driveway
with his hands on the seat behind
you as he jogged to keep up,
you were just beginning
to think about the benefits
of breaking free and where you would go
when without warning he let go
of the seat and you sailed
down the drive and onto the sidewalk
and you no longer cared
that the bike wasn't new
or that it was blue like a boy's or even
where this wild ride would take you,
because you knew
this was just the beginning
of freedom, of leaving home
on your own steam.

November

Big Things in Small Packages

What to read:

Sarah Freligh, "December"
Eamon Grennan, "Gone"
Jane Kenyon, "Not Writing"
Meghan O'Rourke, "Navesink"

I have a great love of short poems—I call this class Big Things in Small Packages because there is so much one can get into just a few careful words. One trick I have for limiting the length of a poem is to use an acrostic. Here's an untitled example:

Bursts of
Irritating one-upmanship
Reverberating in my dreams
Driving
Sleep away. It's
Only 4 a.m.
Now what?
Grrr.

It's a bit like a riddle, in which you find the answer by reading the first letter of each line. I love how the form forces you to make word choices that you otherwise would never have found. Pat used his mother's name to honor her as a woman who had done some powerful community organizing. Note how important a title can be, enabling the poem itself to be short. Also note the image at the end.

PROMPT

Write an acrostic about now, using one word—perhaps someone's name. Begin by writing the word or name down the left margin of your paper. Concrete nouns tend to work best. The lines can be short, but you'll probably want to use more than one word per line, or it will hark back to elementary school writing.

Politicking Parent
Patrick W. Gibson

Pushy until all goals
end in triumph and her
gains spread amongst a block, whose residents
gathered at the house adorned in
yellow roses against stoic flushed brick

PROMPT

Sometimes you need to write a lot of words to discover which ones you need. Try this. Free-write something you've observed of nature in the last few weeks—ants, a tree, an animal—write with as many details as you can summon—don't worry about grammar or spelling or beautiful language—no ongoing revision, just write.

Read "December" by Sarah Freligh and "Not Writing" by Jane Kenyon. Notice all that is contained in these small vessels. How does the title function? How does the title eliminate the need for so much explanation?

Now take a 10-minute break—go wash some dishes or dust a cabinet or sweep a floor. Then come back and gather your free-write into one beautiful sentence of description, beginning with a preposition such as before, after, on, along, despite.

Divide it into a few short lines. Give it an evocative title.

Taking Leave
Linda Gail Francis

After dinner, laughing along with the others,
she places her dishes in the sink,
leaves by the big screen door,
checks the sky—clear this evening—
strolls down the hill to the lake's edge,
sighs the canoe through the mud
along the shore, checks the water—
a silk scarf of blue and gold
against the silhouette of cabins
from across the water—
tightens her core, steps in with care,
creates a ripple with the oar
as she gently pushes off.

PROMPT

Write about someone you have lost in some way. Write for 10 minutes, finding an image to connect them to—a flower or an animal or an ocean they loved. Follow the same rules in the prior prompt about writing without self-revision.

Read "Navesink" by Meghan O'Rourke and "Gone" by Eamon Grennan. Think about why they included their images, and how they barely mentioned the person lost, yet gave us a sense of the person.

Again, do something in your body for 10 minutes, then gather your writing into one sentence.

My Mother's Basement
Patrick W. Gibson

A fly rests on the basement floor,
in the corner amongst dried webs
and upside down with wings still,
antenna pointed at spaces where
Christmas ornaments ranged,
children ran, projects started, stopped,
and never started again,
stagnant, like the fly.

December

More Big Things in Small Packages

What to read:

Natalie Goldberg, *Three Simple Lines*
Elizabeth Spires, "Small as a Seed"

*B*orrowing is a thing in poetry. Forms like sonnets and sestinas came about because someone wrote that way and others thought it was a good idea and copied and developed it—the sonnet is still developing because we keep borrowing ideas from one another and adding our own touches. I love the form of "Small as a Seed" by Elizabeth Spires, so I created this prompt. We read the poem as a class, and talked about word use in the second stanza—how "fall" changes meaning, how the speaker subtly enters the poem.

Pat, reeling from a school shooting near his home, found poetry using a quote he decidedly did not love.

PROMPT

>———→

Take a short quote you love. Play with the syntax of it in the lines of your first stanza. Let yourself enter the second stanza.

No More
Patrick W. Gibson

"No discipline was warranted." – Tim Throne, Oxford School Superintendent, as quoted in *The Detroit News*, December 2, 2021.

No tests aced only growth arrested.
No schoolwork only scatter.
No classmate rapport only student erected barricades.
No pep rally only screaming.
No bells only sirens.

As I watch the horrors scroll on screen and tablet,
and hear firsthand the terror,
I pray comfort. Wish spring witness cold.
No more violence only flowers.
No more loss, only love, from me and to the families, to Oxford and Michigan.

Sara used a quote she loved and let some rhyme slip in.

Resilience

Sara Palmer

"I will keep broken things" ~ Alice Walker

I will keep my fragile bones,
I will keep my shattered heart,
I will keep beautiful and broken parts.
I will keep them while they mend.
I will keep them, though they break again.

Oh, I dread the slip of time,
Chill of illness, pain, decline.
And yet, each healing moment is sublime!
I will keep the crooked scars that tell my story,
I will keep these broken things that sing of human glory.

I am no haiku expert, but I'm learning and appreciating it more and more. A quick reading of haiku is a bit like glancing at a postcard depicting a major work of art—"oh, that's nice."

It takes time to let the work settle; this is why it's wonderful to read haiku (and any poetry) with a group. If you don't have a poetry discussion group, I recommend Natalie Goldberg's new book *Three Simple Lines*. Having the haiku separated by her prose helps you appreciate it, solo.

After talking about some classic haiku and whether we should stick with the classic 5-7-5 syllable/line form (answer: it's totally optional, worth trying if your writing tends to be too wordy), I had everyone write a haiku based on Robert Frost's poem, "Dust of Snow." With a shared image, we could appreciate each other's style and word choice even more.

Here are some of ours. First, look at one by Julia, who took the prompt literally and delivered the 5-7-5 form.

PROMPT

>>———→

Read "Dust of Snow" or another short poem with a strong image and write a haiku based on it. Keep it to 17 syllables or less.

Untitled
Julia W. Prentice

Crow touching pine branch
Sifting snowfall turns my mood
Saving a ruined day

$\mathcal{S}$ara shared two poems using this imagery.

Untitled
Sara Palmer

1.

Snow dust falling
from a pine sprinkles
light into my mind.

2.

White snow, green pine
in a moment
my heart is opened.

Linda changed the image a bit and gave us two versions. There is lots of craft in writing this spare form well. It's a great discipline for honing your language and your thinking about image.

Untitled
Linda Gail Francis

Original 5-7-5 form:

Crumbled frost resting
just outside the front door's warmth
doomed and sparkling bright.

Stripped-down, form-free version:

On the ground
a patch of frost,
doomed and sparkling.

Contributors

Claudia Cameron received MAs in art therapy and clinical social work. She has practiced clinical social work and art therapy with children, families, and women for 40 years. Her lifelong passion for art shifted in the past 20 years from photography to painting. She has studied with various nationally known painters including Tamara Sigler and Ruth Pettus. Claudia paints with acrylics on canvas and paper. Her work has been exhibited in juried and nonjuried shows, including the Waldorf School (2004), The Hoffberger Gallery (2007), the Myerberg Center (2007, 2010, 2014), The Gordon Center (2008), The Towson Arts Collective (2008), the Women's Artists' Forum (2010), the Lodge at Woodloch (2009, 2016), and Sascha's (2012). Her paintings are in private collections from Florida to Rhode Island.

Linda Gail Francis has always enjoyed words, whether they're flying through the air or sitting still on the page. Following earlier experiences as a waitress, teacher, and radio host, she has worked for many years as an editor. She loves podcasts, public radio, jazz (especially live!) and most other types of music, water aerobics, and doing what she can to help. She has been writing to think (and thinking to write) for most of her life; for the past 10 years or so her focus has been on poetry. She lives in Baltimore with her partner and their sweet cat and is the author of the self-published collection *Coming Across: Poems and Lunch*.

Patrick W. Gibson is a Metro Detroit-based poet and writer. His work has been published by *The Flexible Persona*, Medusa's Laugh, Wraparound South, Dark Ink, Fiction Attic, ARTIFEX, University of Michigan's *Bear River Review*, *Potato Soup Journal*, *EKL Review*, and HellBound Books. He has been featured on the "Ripples in Space" podcast. Pat is querying his first novel and beginning a second. When not writing he likes to read and spend time with family.

Jessica Gregg is a single mother who came to poetry because she didn't have time to write anything longer—then she got hooked. She is a former Yellow Arrow Publishing Writer-in-Residence, and her chapbook, *News from This Lonesome City*, was published in 2019. "Poetry is Life" helped sustain her writing practice during the pandemic and for that, she is immensely grateful.

Sara Palmer is a retired psychologist and author of four nonfiction books on coping with illness, disability, and caregiving. A poet since childhood, she now hones her craft in classes and writing groups. Her first published poem appeared in *Yellow Arrow Journal* in 2020. Two of her poems were included in *Fractured Hearts: Multi-faith Words of Hope and Healing*, edited and published by Rabbi Debra Smith in 2021. Sara lives in Baltimore, Maryland. She is a volunteer board member for Yellow Arrow. She enjoys walking, reading, spending time with friends, and visiting her grandchildren as often as possible.

Julia W. Prentice grew up in Connecticut and has been writing poetry since her teen years. She graduated from Clark University, with a BA in Foreign Language & Literature. She currently lives in Charlotte, North Carolina with her soulmate and their furry companion. An ASL interpreter, peer supporter of persons with mental health challenges, and knitter, crafter, and singer, Julia puts her passion into all of these. She is published in many anthologies, was a finalist in the Poet's Billow Atlantis award (2015) and had a poem nominated for the Pushcart Prize (2017). You may reach her through email, jmwp1972@gmail.com, or on Facebook and read her blog IAMSTARLIGHT.

Ann Quinn's chapbook *Final Deployment* was published by Finishing Line Press in 2018. Her poetry has appeared in *Poet Lore*, *Potomac Review*, *Little Patuxent Review*, *Yellow Arrow Journal*, and others. Ann holds an MFA from Pacific Lutheran University, is poetry editor for *Yellow Arrow Journal*, and lives in Catonsville, Maryland. She teaches for Yellow Arrow and for the Writer's Center in Bethesda, Maryland, and has a loyal following of students of all ages and places in their writing journey. Ann states: "There is nothing like the feeling of a poem being born into the world through your own hands, but as satisfying for me is the joy of seeing a poem come to the world through one of my student's hands. The world comes a little more clearly into focus the more we look at it together through the lens of poetry." Learn more at annquinn.net.

Patti Ross graduated from Washington, D.C.'s Duke Ellington School for the Performing Arts and The American University. After graduation, several of her journalist pieces were published in the *Washington Times* and the Rural America newspapers. Retiring from a career in technology, Patti has rediscovered her love of writing and shares her voice as the spoken word artist little pi. Her poems are published in the *Pen In Hand Journal*, PoetryXHunger website, and Oyster River Pages: *Composite Dreams Issue*, among others. You can find Patti at littlepisuniverse.com or on Facebook and Instagram. Her debut chapbook, *St. Paul Street Provocations*, was published by Yellow Arrow in 2021.

Nikita Rimal Sharma currently resides in Baltimore, Maryland with her husband and dog, Stone, and works at B'More Clubhouse, a community-based mental health nonprofit. She is originally from Kathmandu, Nepal. Nikita is a typical homebody who gets a lot of joy from slow running, short hikes, reading, and deep thoughts. Her journey with poetry started when she took the first class organized by Yellow Arrow taught by the lovely Ann Quinn. Since then, she has had the opportunity to publish in *Yellow Arrow Journal* **(Re)Formation** from fall 2020. Nikita's chapbook, *The most beautiful garden*, will be published by Yellow Arrow in 2022.

Jobie Townshend-Zellner's love of poetry began in high school, when she received a gift of a compact anthology, *One Hundred and One Famous Poems*, designed to "enrich, ennoble, encourage." It accompanied her solitary nature walks in the hills around her Southern California childhood home, and to this day remains in her library, now housed in San Diego. Jobie finds that weaving words into the fabric of poetry brings the threads of life together. She has self-published two soft bound books and is immensely grateful to Ann Quinn for including some of her poems in *Poetry is Life*.

Image Credits

January	"Kitchen Scene" – Linda Gail Francis
February	"Clouds Parting" – Jobie Townshend-Zellner
March	"Fillmore" – Patrick W. Gibson
April	"Castle" – Patrick W. Gibson
May	"Lotus" – Jobie Townshend-Zellner
June	"Tree Lake Sun" – Jobie Townshend-Zellner
July	"Teacup" – Jobie Townshend-Zellner
August	"Luna" – Rose Ocone
September	"City Morning Out the Window" – Linda Gail Francis
October	"Self-Shadow in Water" – Ann Quinn
November	"Trunk" – Patrick W. Gibson
December	"Branch" – Patrick W. Gibson

Thank you for supporting independent publishing.

Yellow Arrow Publishing is a nonprofit supporting writers that identify as women. Visit YellowArrowPublishing.com for information on our publications, workshops, and writing opportunities.

CPSIA information can be obtained
at www.ICGtesting.com
Printed in the USA
BVHW081743110222
628354BV00001B/67